WHAT·DO·WE·KNOW
ABOUT
CHRISTIANITY·?

CAROL WATSON

MACDONALD YOUNG BOOKS

First published in 1997 by
Macdonald Young Books

© Macdonald Young Books 1997,
an imprint of Wayland Publishers Ltd

Macdonald Young Books
61 Western Road
Hove
East Sussex BN3 1JD

Designer and illustrator: Celia Hart
Commissioning editor: Hazel Songhurst
Editor: Debbie Fox
Picture research: Jane Taylor

Printed in Hong Kong by Wing King Tong

A CIP catalogue record for this book
is available from the British Library

ISBN: 0 7500 1981 6

Endpapers: These stained glass windows show two
scenes from the New Testament, *The Annunciation* is on
the left and *The Nativity* is on the right. They were made
in CE1491 and are in a church in Italy.

. CONTENTS .

·WHAT·IS·A· CHRISTIAN?

A Christian is someone who believes in and follows the teachings of Jesus Christ. Jesus was a Jew who was born about 2000 years ago in Bethlehem, in the country then known as Palestine. Jesus lived for 33 years before being crucified by the Romans who occupied the land. Christians believe that Jesus rose from the dead and appeared to his disciples to show everyone that there is another life with one, eternal, loving God. Christianity has spread across the world and there are now over 1500 million Christians worldwide.

THE SPREAD OF CHRISTIANITY

These African Christians are singing and worshipping God together. The Romans first took Christianity to north Africa in the second century CE. The Romans also spread Christianity across their vast empire, throughout the Mediterranean countries to Europe, Persia and India. In the 10th century CE Greek monks introduced Christianity to Russia, and from the 16th century onwards the Spanish, Portuguese and English spread the faith to North and South America.

EVANGELISTS

An evangelist is someone who enthusiastically spreads the message of Christianity to as many people as possible in order to convert them to the faith. Christians want other people to have the opportunity of knowing about Jesus Christ, so that they can choose to change their lives if they wish to. Most evangelists are people who speak or preach to large gatherings of people. Some Christians evangelise by means of television, radio, books and tapes. In this photograph a world famous American evangelist, Billy Graham, is preaching to thousands of people who have come to hear about God. Billy Graham has held rallies in most of the major cities of the world and is thought to have converted millions of people to Christianity.

Number of Christians (millions)

- over 100
- 50 – 100
- 10 – 50
- 1 – 10

THE CHRISTIAN WORLD

This map is a guide to the distribution of Christians in the world. Only Brazil and the USA have over 100 million Christians because the population of each country is very high. However, in the Philippines, for example, there are nearly 63 million Christians, which represents 90% of the population. In Mexico there are nearly 93 million Christians, representing 95% of the population.

DIFFERENT BRANCHES OF CHRISTIANITY

Although all Christians are followers of Christ and use the Bible, there are some differences in belief and practice. There are three main branches of Christianity – Roman Catholic, Protestant and Orthodox. Orthodox Christianity originated in Greece and the East. Roman Catholicism and Protestantism originated in the West. Today there are all kinds of Christians all over the world.

CHRISTIAN WORK

Christians believe that the most important thing is to love God and to live their lives for God's purpose. They believe God has given them talents to work for the good of others and to spread the gospel of Jesus Christ. Monks, nuns, priests and ministers devote their lives to serving people. This nun is called Sister Angela. She is visiting one of the patients at a London hospital. Sister Angela belongs to an order of nuns that help and visit poor and sick people in the area where they live.

TIMELINE

EVENTS IN CHRISTIANITY

BCE = Before the Common Era = BC (Before the birth of Jesus Christ)

CE = The Common Era = AD

AD = *Anno Domini* (the Year of our Lord) = the years after the birth of Christ.
When the first historians worked out the date of the birth of Jesus Christ they miscalculated by four years. The correct date for the birth of Christ is therefore 4BC, not AD1.

61BCE	4BCE	*c.* CE26	*c.* CE29	*c.* CE29 (Three days later)	*c.* CE29 (Forty days later)	*c.* CE29 (Ten days later)
The mighty Roman Empire had spread across the Mediterranean and occupied Judea (part of Palestine).	Jesus Christ, the Son of God, the Messiah, was born into a Jewish family in a stable in Bethlehem, in Judea.	Jesus began his work of teaching people about God in an area called Galilee. He chose twelve followers, or disciples (later called apostles), to help him.	The Jewish leaders plotted against Jesus. They handed him over to the Romans who executed him. He was put to death by crucifixion.	Jesus Christ rose from the dead and appeared to his disciples. This is called the 'Resurrection'.	Jesus went to heaven to be with God. This is called the 'Ascension'.	Fifty days after the Resurrection the Holy Spirit came upon Jesus' disciples on the day of Pentecost. The Early Church began.

Roman soldier

Star of Bethlehem

CE1540	CE1535	CE1517	CE1300	CE1209	CE1096	CE1054
Ignatius Loyola founded the Society of Jesus – The Jesuits.	William Tyndale's English translation of the original Greek and Hebrew Bible was first allowed in England.	Martin Luther began the Reformation in Europe. The Protestant branch of Christianity was established.	Christianity had reached Iceland, China and Russia.	St Francis of Assisi created his order of the Franciscan monks. Soon after this St Clare founded her order of nuns.	The Crusades began. These were holy wars during which Christians and Muslims fought each other to capture the city of Jerusalem.	The final split between eastern (Orthodox) and western (Roman Catholic) Christian churches took place.

CE1543	
Henry VIII made himself head of the church in England.	

Henry VIII

Martin Luther

CE1549	CE1611	CE1620	CE1703	CE1792	CE1858	CE1910
The first English Book of Common Prayer was used.	The Authorised Version of the Bible was published.	In order to worship God as they wished, English Puritans, called 'The Pilgrim Fathers', sailed from England to America.	The birth of John Wesley – the founder of Methodism.	The first missionary society in England was founded by the Baptists.	The start of the visions of the Virgin Mary at Lourdes.	The first World Missionary Conference was held.

c. CE33	CE47–60	CE60–65	CE65–100	CE70
Saul (Paul), who had persecuted the followers of Christ, had a vision of Jesus and was converted to Christianity.	The time of Paul's missionary journeys and writing of the epistles. Followers of Jesus Christ became known as Christians.	The persecution of the Christians by the Roman Emperor, Nero. Many Christians died horrific deaths as martyrs.	The time when the gospels of the New Testament were written.	Jerusalem was taken over by the Romans, who destroyed the Second Temple.

CE100
By this time at least 25,000 Christians had been executed for their beliefs.

Paul's ship

CE800	CE313	c. CE300	c. CE200	CE180
The Pope made the Emperor Charlemagne the first Holy Roman Emperor.	Constantine the Great allowed the Christians in the Roman Empire to worship freely.	Roman Christianity came to Britain.	Celtic Christianity came to Britain.	By this time Christianity had spread across the Roman Empire, to Persia, North Africa and India.

A statue of Charlemagne

Woman priest

was held. CE1948	Amsterdam. CE1962–5	Church. CE1968	CE1986	CE1993
The World Council of Churches was founded in	The Vatican Council began a series of reforms of the Roman Catholic	The World Council of Churches formed the Ecumenical Movement in order to bring more unity to the Christian church.	The Pope, Archbishop of Canterbury and leaders of other faiths met in Assisi, Italy, to pray for peace.	The first women were ordained as priests in the Church of England.

THE MESSIAH

The prophets of ancient Israel foretold that God would send a saviour, or special leader, into the world to rescue them from their enemies. Throughout their history the Jewish people have longed for this saviour or 'Messiah' to come. The Jews believe that the Messiah has not yet come into the world. Christians believe that Jesus Christ was the Messiah that God promised to the Jews. They believe that Jesus did not come into the world to replace what the Jews believe in, but to

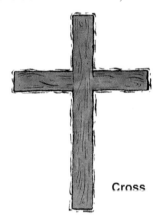

Cross

fulfil it.

THE SIGN OF THE CROSS

Jesus Christ died by being nailed to a wooden cross. This was an agonising death, which caused the maximum amount of pain. Christians believe that Jesus' death was a sacrifice so that everyone could draw close to God and be forgiven. The sign of the cross has therefore become a symbol of suffering and sacrifice. The cross now also appears as a sign of help or aid for many

Christians believe that Jesus Christ was the Son of God who came into the world to save people from their sins and show them the way to God. They believe that if people are sorry for what they have done wrong, God forgives them and offers them a new life with him in this world and also in heaven after they have died. The name Christ comes from the Greek word *Khristos*, which means the same as the word Messiah in Hebrew. Christians also believe in the Holy Trinity – God the Father, God the Son and God the Holy Spirit.

THE BIRTH OF JESUS CHRIST

Jesus was born around 4 BCE. His mother and father, Mary and Joseph, were a Jewish couple who were descendants of the Jewish King David. Before Mary married Joseph, an angel of God appeared to her and told Mary that she was going to have a child who was the Son of God. This picture is called *The Annunciation* because it shows the Angel Gabriel announcing the news to Mary. The angel told Mary that God had chosen her to give birth to the Messiah.

In the Bible the angel says to Mary, "You are to name the child Jesus. He will be great and will be called the Son of the most High ... His kingdom will never end." The same angel also appeared to Joseph to reassure him that Mary's pregnancy was a miracle. So Joseph married Mary and the baby Jesus was born. He lived with his parents in Nazareth and worked as a carpenter until it was time for him to begin God's work.

JESUS TEACHES AND HEALS THE SICK

When he was about 30 years old Jesus began to teach people about God. He chose twelve followers who were known as his 'disciples' (later called apostles). Accompanied by these men, Jesus travelled throughout Palestine performing miracles, healing the sick and telling people about God. Jesus told the people how God would provide for their needs if they would believe and trust in him and obey his laws. Everywhere Jesus went crowds flocked to listen to him teach. This mosaic shows a picture of Jesus Christ blessing his followers. Just beneath Jesus you can also see some of the twelve apostles. The rings around their heads are halos which the artist has used to show they are holy people chosen by God.

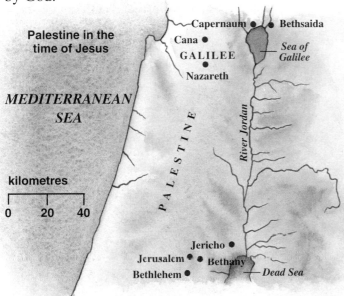

Palestine in the time of Jesus

Capernaum • • Bethsaida
Cana •
GALILEE
Sea of Galilee
Nazareth

MEDITERRANEAN SEA

PALESTINE

River Jordan

kilometres
0   20   40

Jericho •
Jerusalem • • Bethany
Bethlehem •   — Dead Sea

PALESTINE

This was the name given by the Romans to the ancient Jewish land of Canaan (later called Israel). Jesus was born and spent his life teaching in this part of the world.

 THE TWO GREAT COMMANDMENTS

Jesus gave his followers two commandments or laws to guide them. " Love the Lord, your God with all your heart, and with all your soul, and with all your strength and with all your mind," and "Love each other as you love yourselves."

HELPING OTHERS

Christians aim to live their lives the way Jesus instructed them, caring for other people around them, and using their God-given talents to spread Jesus' teaching. Many Christians work to help the poor and underprivileged throughout the world. This photograph shows a relief worker from an Irish aid agency who is working to help the people of Somalia suffering from famine. Wherever they are, and however they work, Christians pray to God to ask for guidance in the way they should behave and in the decisions they make.

· HOW · DID · CHRISTIANITY · BEGIN ? ·

Christianity began when the followers of Jesus carried on his teachings after he had died. Before he left them, Jesus told his disciples to go into the world to tell everyone about forgiveness. "I am the way, the truth and the life," he said. "No one can reach the Father unless they believe in me." Jesus told his apostles that God would send his Holy Spirit to give them the strength and support to carry on his work. After the day of Pentecost (see page 23), the apostles did as he had commanded. Thousands of people became disciples too. At first they were called followers of 'the Way'. Later they became known as 'Christians'.

THE FIRST CHRISTIAN MARTYR

One of the first Christians was a man called Stephen. God gave him great power and he began to preach and heal the sick. People flocked to hear Stephen until he was arrested by the Jewish high priests. They were so enraged at the things Stephen said to them that they falsely accused him of speaking against God. Stephen was dragged outside the city walls and was stoned to death. As he lay dying, Stephen cried out, "Lord, forgive them for what they are doing." In this painting Stephen lies on the ground as the crowds hurl rocks and boulders at him. Nearby other Christians watch in dismay as they see Stephen die. Sitting in the foreground a man points towards the accused. He is looking after the cloaks of those taking part. This man is Saul, who was one of the Jewish leaders.

 MARTYRS

Martyrs are people who die for their faith. Since the death of Stephen, many Christians throughout history have also died because of their belief in Jesus Christ. Even today, Christians in some parts of the world are persecuted for their beliefs.

THE CONVERSION OF ST PAUL

Saul was one of the main ringleaders who set out to stop the spread of Christianity. He was determined to kill or persecute all the Christians he could find. Saul travelled far and wide searching for followers of 'the Way'. One day, on the road to Damascus, he had a vision of Christ in the sky. This painting shows Saul falling from his horse as he sees Jesus and hears his words, " Saul, Saul, why are you persecuting me?" Saul was blinded by the vision of Christ and had to be led into town. There a Christian prayed for him and his sight was restored. After that Saul became a Christian too. His name was changed to Paul and he became one of the greatest of Jesus' apostles. He is now known as Saint Paul.

I	Jesus
X	Christ
Θ	God's
Y	Son
Σ	Saviour

ΙΧΘΥΣ

SECRET CODE

The Romans persecuted the Christians and it became dangerous for them to meet. So the Christians devised a secret code. They drew half a fish in the sand. If a person completed the fish, they knew he or she was a believer too. Under the fish symbol the Christians wrote the Greek word fish, Ι Χ Θ Υ Σ. These letters stood for: Jesus Christ God's Son Saviour.

MISSIONARIES

Paul became the first Christian missionary. This is someone who travels to places where people have never heard about Jesus Christ. Paul spread Christianity throughout the Mediterranean into Greece, Turkey and Rome. Christians want everyone to be given the opportunity of having a new life with God. Since Paul, other missionaries have taken Christianity all over the world. This photograph shows a priest and a nun giving Mass to people in Africa. Today the Christian faith is spreading rapidly in many African countries.

There are different branches of Christianity because some Christians worship in different ways. For a long time the first Christians were persecuted by the Romans until one of the Roman Emperors became a Christian too. The Emperor Constantine stopped the persecution of the Christians and allowed them to worship freely. He built a new Christian capital city in the East called Constantinople (now Istanbul). The Christian faith was then able to spread throughout the Roman Empire into Europe. Eventually Christianity became the state religion and the vast empire of Rome became known as the Holy Roman Empire.

THE GREAT DIVIDE

This diagram illustrates how the different branches of Christianity came about. The different regions of Christianity had leaders called patriarchs (bishops). They were supposed to have equal power, but the Patriarchs of Rome and Constantinople were given more power than the others. These two men argued over points of worship and belief and so the Patriarch of Rome separated his church and it became known as the Roman Catholic faith.

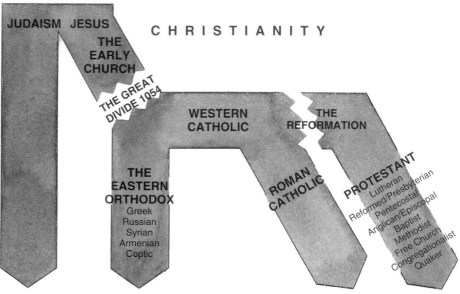

JUDAISM JESUS CHRISTIANITY

THE EARLY CHURCH

THE GREAT DIVIDE 1054

WESTERN CATHOLIC

THE REFORMATION

THE EASTERN ORTHODOX
Greek
Russian
Syrian
Armenian
Coptic

ROMAN CATHOLIC

PROTESTANT
Lutheran
Reformed/Presbyterian
Pentecostal
Anglican/Episcopal
Baptist
Methodist
Free Church
Congregationalist
Quaker

ROMAN CATHOLICS

The word 'catholic' means univ: sal. The western, Latin-speaking part of the Roman Empire saw itself as the continuation of the true church and used the name 'Catholic'. The Roman Catholic headquarters are in the Vatican in Rome and the patriarch became known as the Pope. In this photograph the Pope is speaking from the balcony of the Vatican to the crowds gathered below.

THE ORTHODOX CHURCH

The word 'orthodox' means 'right belief or worship'. The eastern, Greek-speaking part of the church also saw itself as the true faith and called itself 'Orthodox'. For many years the head of this church was the Patriarch of Constantinople and the services were conducted in Greek. The Greek Orthodox monks spread the faith to Russia and Slav countries, so there are now Russian patriarchs too. This photograph is of Alexei II, Patriarch of Moscow. He is the head of the Orthodox Church in Russia.

 THE VIRGIN MARY

Both Roman Catholics and Orthodox Christians give more emphasis to the Virgin Mary than Protestants. They believe that because she is the mother of Jesus, she has special access to him and can communicate with him on behalf of those who pray to her.

PROTESTANTS

The Christian church continued to spread and change throughout the centuries. Gradually people with strong beliefs began to challenge the way some Roman Catholic priests were behaving. The portrait on the left is of a German monk called Martin Luther. He felt the church had moved away from the teaching of Jesus and he wanted reforms or changes. Luther and others 'protested' about the existing ways of teaching and worship and set up their own form of Christianity. These rebels were called 'Protestants' and this period in history was known as the 'Reformation'. Protestant services were no longer held in Latin but in the common language so that everybody could understand what was being said. Protestants focus on the Bible as the heart of their teaching. There are many groups of Protestants, such as Anglicans, Methodists and Baptists.

·WHAT·IS· CHRISTMAS?·

Christmas is the first festival of the Christian year. It is a joyful celebration when Christians believe God came into the world as a person. This is called the 'Incarnation'. The word Christmas comes from the Old English 'Chrestes Maesses', or 'Christ's Mass'. Roman Catholics and Protestants celebrate Christmas on the 25th December (chosen by the Emperor Constantine to coincide with the Roman sun festival). Eastern Orthodox Christians celebrate the birth of Jesus on the 7th January. No-one knows the exact date of Jesus' birth.

CHRISTIAN FESTIVALS

Christian festivals are closely related to events in the life of Jesus. This chart shows at what time in the Christian year they take place. The dates of the festivals from Lent to Pentecost depend on the date of Easter, which is not a fixed date, but varies from year to year.

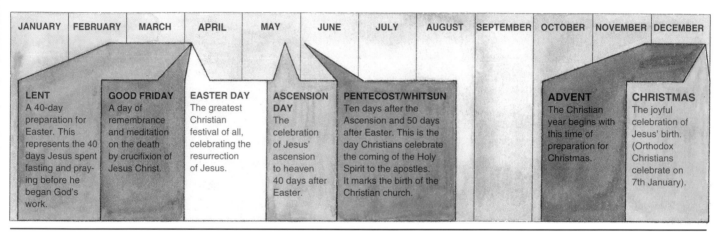

JANUARY	FEBRUARY	MARCH	APRIL	MAY	JUNE	JULY	AUGUST	SEPTEMBER	OCTOBER	NOVEMBER	DECEMBER

LENT
A 40-day preparation for Easter. This represents the 40 days Jesus spent fasting and praying before he began God's work.

GOOD FRIDAY
A day of remembrance and meditation on the death by crucifixion of Jesus Christ.

EASTER DAY
The greatest Christian festival of all, celebrating the resurrection of Jesus.

ASCENSION DAY
The celebration of Jesus' ascension to heaven 40 days after Easter.

PENTECOST/WHITSUN
Ten days after the Ascension and 50 days after Easter. This is the day Christians celebrate the coming of the Holy Spirit to the apostles. It marks the birth of the Christian church.

ADVENT
The Christian year begins with this time of preparation for Christmas.

CHRISTMAS
The joyful celebration of Jesus' birth. (Orthodox Christians celebrate on 7th January).

ADVENT
The word Advent means 'coming'. This is the time of preparation for Christmas when Christians meditate on the meaning of Jesus' birth. They also look forward to the Second Coming of Jesus, when they believe he will return to bring God's justice to the world. Advent begins four Sundays before Christmas. In many churches, each Sunday, one of four candles is lit. These children are lighting the first of four Advent candles. The one in the middle represents Jesus and is lit on Christmas Day.

THE BIRTH OF JESUS

The Bible tells the story of Jesus' birth. Just before Jesus was born, Joseph and his wife Mary, the mother of Jesus, had to make a long journey from their home town of Nazareth to a place called Bethlehem. By the time they arrived there was nowhere left to stay. So Mary and Joseph found shelter in a stable. That night, Mary had her baby. She wrapped him up warmly and used the animal's manger as a cot for him to sleep in. The night of his birth, angels of God appeared to local shepherds and told them that the 'Saviour', or 'Messiah', had been born. The shepherds went to worship the baby Jesus. Meanwhile, far away in the East, wise men, who were probably astronomers, had been studying a new star in the sky. It meant that a new king had been born. The wise men travelled for days to find the place where the star was. There they found Jesus. They worshipped him and gave him gifts of gold, frankincense and myrhh. The Christmas crib scene shows models of Mary, Joseph and the shepherds worshipping the baby Jesus in the manger.

Christmas crib

CHRISTMAS WORSHIP

On Christmas Eve or Christmas Day Christians go to church to worship and give thanks to God for sending his Son into the world. These children are leaving church in Kazakhstan after a Christmas service.

CHRISTMAS PRESENTS

Everyone looks forward to Christmas as a time of giving and receiving presents. Christians, like these people in the photograph, give each other presents on the day of Christ's birth because they remember that God gave Jesus as a gift to the world.

·WHAT·IS· ·EASTER?·

Easter Day is the most important festival for Christians as it celebrates the day Jesus Christ rose from the dead. The 40 days leading up to Easter Day are called 'Lent'. This is a time of repentance when Christians ask for forgiveness for their sins. The week before Easter is called 'Holy Week' and begins with Palm Sunday, the day the crowds welcomed Jesus as he rode into Jerusalem on a donkey. The Last Supper (see pages 28 and 39) is commemorated on Holy Thursday, which is sometimes called 'Maundy Thursday'. Good Friday is the day Jesus was crucified.

LENT

The first day of Lent is Ash Wednesday. In some churches the priest uses ash to make the sign of the cross on the forehead of each worshipper. This is to symbolise that they have repented of their sins and received forgiveness. During Lent many Christians remember the time Jesus spent fasting (going without food) and praying before he began to do God's work. Some Christians also fast in some way at this time.

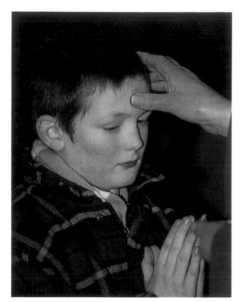

PALM SUNDAY

The Sunday before he was crucified, the crowds waved palm branches to welcome Jesus into Jerusalem. To celebrate Palm Sunday, in some churches Christians are given dried palm leaves. These are folded into the shape of a cross like the one in the drawing.

A palm cross

THE LAST SUPPER

The night before he was crucified, Jesus and his disciples had a final meal together. This is called 'The Last Supper'. Before they began the meal, Jesus knelt and washed his disciples' feet. This job was usually reserved for the humblest servant and Jesus was doing it to show that he and his followers were to 'serve' (help) others. In this painting, the apostle Peter is reluctant to let his master do such a mundane job. But Jesus insists that Peter cannot be one of his followers unless he allows it.

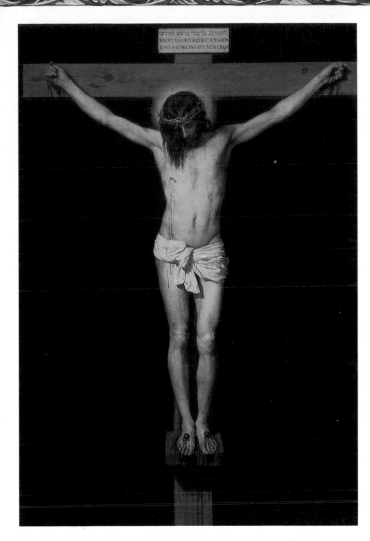

GOOD FRIDAY

For Christians this is a day of fasting and sorrow. The name 'Good' probably meant 'God's' Friday, or possibly started at a time when the word 'good' meant 'holy'. This is the day Christians remember the crucifixion of Jesus Christ. Jesus was put to death because the Jewish high priests felt threatened by his teaching and so they plotted against him. They handed him over to the Romans, who sentenced him to death. The Roman soldiers whipped and mocked Jesus. They made him wear a crown made of thorns and nicknamed him 'The King of the Jews'. Then Jesus was nailed to a wooden cross and left to die, hanging in the heat of the sun. This painting shows Jesus on the cross. The sign above his head says 'King of the Jews'. The Bible tells how, as he was dying, Jesus asked God to forgive those executing him. When he was dead, Jesus' body was taken to a tomb. There it was wrapped in cloth, and a huge stone was rolled across the entrance to the tomb. The greatest sacrifice anyone can make is to die for someone else. Christians believe Jesus died so that all people could receive forgiveness and have a relationship with God.

EASTER DAY

For Christians this is the most joyful day in their calendar. It is when Christians remember Jesus' resurrection, or rising from the dead. They believe that three days after he died, Jesus rose from the dead and appeared to his followers many times. They also believe that he showed that when people die, it is not the end and that there is an everlasting life with God for those that believe in him. This painting shows Jesus appearing to his disciples. One of the apostles, Thomas, (sometimes known as Doubting Thomas) said he would only believe that Jesus had risen if he could touch the wounds made by the nails and sword that had finally killed him. Jesus appeared to Thomas so that he could see for himself. On Easter Day churches are decorated with flowers and Christians rejoice, sing and give each other presents. Many people remember Easter Day by giving each other Easter eggs. Christians see these as a symbol of the new and everlasting life that Jesus gave to all believers.

·WHAT·ARE· THE·OTHER CHRISTIAN· FESTIVALS?

The other two main festivals of the Christian calendar that commemorate the life of Jesus Christ are Ascension and Pentecost. These are the last of the festivals that celebrate events recorded in the Bible. Other minor festivals celebrated by some Christians are feast days and saints days, such as All Saints Day and Harvest Festival. These festivals are a mixture of local tradition and customs mixed with Christian prayer and song. The festivals are celebrated in different ways throughout the world.

THE ASCENSION

The Bible describes how the Ascension took place 40 days after Jesus Christ rose from the dead. During that time Jesus appeared to his disciples and talked to them many times. He told them what he wanted them to do after he had gone to heaven to join God. Jesus said, "Don't ever forget that, although you can't see me, I am always with you." After he had said this, Jesus lifted up his hands to bless the apostles. And, as he blessed them he was taken up to heaven and disappeared from their sight. This painting shows Jesus ascending, or going up, into heaven to be with God. While the disciples stared upwards, two angels appeared amongst them. "Why are you looking up at the sky?" they said. "Jesus has been taken from you now, but one day he will come back in the same way as he went to heaven."

PENTECOST

Ten days after the Ascension was the day of Pentecost, sometimes called 'Whitsun'. Christians believe on that day God sent his Holy Spirit to Jesus' followers. The apostles were filled with joy and inspiration and sang songs of praise to God. They also found they were able to preach in foreign languages, sometimes called 'speaking in tongues', so they could tell people from different countries all about Jesus. The Christians on the right are called Pentecostals because their form of worship concentrates on experiencing the presence of the Holy Spirit and praising God out loud.

GIFTS OF THE SPIRIT

The spontaneous worship practised by the Pentecostals has spread into other churches. The Christians pictured here are 'Charismatics'. As they praise God they lift their hands towards heaven to receive the Holy Spirit. The word 'charismatic' means 'gift'. Like Pentecostals, these Christians believe they are using the gifts given to them by God through his Holy Spirit. Some pray for people to be healed, others prophesy (foretell events) or have religious visions, and many believe they have the ability to 'speak in tongues'.

SAINTS AND SAINTS DAYS

The Roman Catholic Church declares some very holy people to be saints after a long process called 'canonisation'. Usually there have to have been two miracles performed through that person's relationship with God. Often people who have died for their faith are made saints too. Many saints have their own days of the year on which they are remembered. Often this is the day the saint died. Statues of saints might be carried through the streets in processions.

This is a picture of Saint Francis of Assisi who lived from 1181 to 1226. Saint Francis was an Italian preacher and monk who had a vision of God that changed his life. He set up an order of monks called 'Franciscans', who devoted their lives to the poor, sick and helpless and who had particular respect for animals.

WHAT·IS·THE CHRISTIANS' ·HOLY·BOOK?·

The Christians' holy book is the Bible. Christians believe that the Bible is God's teaching written down to guide people in the way they live. It starts with how the world began and ends with a prediction of the future. Although it looks like one book, the Bible is really a collection of 66 books that were written down by different people at different times. The books include history, drama, poetry, letters, laws and stories of people's lives. There are two main sections in the Bible – the Old Testament and the New Testament.

THE OLD TESTAMENT

The word 'testament' means agreement or promise. The first 39 books of the Bible are in the Old Testament. This tells of God's promise to Abraham and his descendants, the Jewish people. The promise was that if they obeyed and trusted in him, he would always love and protect them. The Old Testament was written on scrolls by the scribes of ancient Israel. The photograph on the left shows a cave in Qumran, near the Dead Sea, in Israel. There, in 1947, an Arab shepherd boy found some ancient scrolls in some old clay pots. These turned out to be priceless copies of parts of the Old Testament and became known as the 'Dead Sea Scrolls'.

SCROLLS

The Old Testament was written down thousands of years ago. In those days very few people could read and write and so educated people called scribes wrote down everything that needed to be recorded. The scribes used reed pens and ink made from charcoal and gum to write on sheets of papyrus (a kind of paper). The sheets were stuck together to make long scrolls.

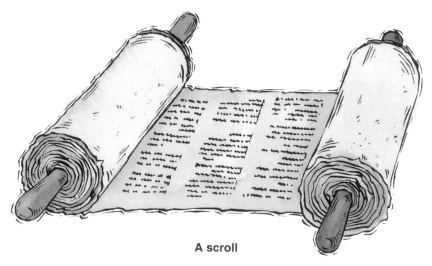

A scroll

THE NEW TESTAMENT

The New Testament is made up of the final 27 books of the Bible. This section is about God's new promise. It tells of how God sent his own son, Jesus, into the world to offer forgiveness and a new life to those who believe and trust in him. The New Testament is a record of Jesus' life and teaching, his crucifixion and resurrection. It tells the story of how the Christian church began and grew, and how Christians believe that Jesus will return to the world. It was written in Greek by the followers of Jesus and members of the early church. This picture shows how the New Testament was written on sheets of parchment bound together at the edges – rather like books today. This was called a 'codex'.

Codex

TRANSLATING THE BIBLE

By CE100 both sections of the Bible had been translated into Greek. The Greek word for books is *biblia*, so that is why they became known as the Bible. The Bible was first translated into Latin, Syriac and Coptic (an ancient Eygptian language). Many of the hand-written versions of the Bible were beautifully decorated by the monks that copied them. This is a photograph of a page from a beautifully illustrated Bible. The first authorised English translation of the Bible was published in 1611. It has now been translated into nearly 2000 languages.

READING THE BIBLE

All Christians read the Bible. It has great importance for many Christians who rely on the Bible as the source of all truth. Christian worship is based on readings and teachings from both the Old and New Testaments. The minister in the photograph is reading aloud a passage from the Bible to the people who have come to worship.

· H O W · D O · CHRISTIANS WORSHIP ?

Christians worship by praying, reading the Bible and singing hymns, or songs of praise, to God. Whenever they can, Christians like to meet together to worship and celebrate their beliefs. Any regular gathering of Christians is called a 'church'. This is also the name given to the buildings in which they meet. Christians may worship together at any time, but the main day for worship is a Sunday. This is the Christian holy day, the day of rest and worship, because that was the day Jesus rose from the dead. Church services are led by a priest, vicar, minister or other leader. Some churches have a formal and very structured way of worshipping, others are informal and spontaneous. In many churches the children go to classes during or after the services. These classes are often called Sunday school.

Altar cross

THE LORD'S SUPPER

An important part of Christian worship is the celebration called Mass, Holy Communion, the Eucharist or the Lord's Supper. Before he was crucified, Jesus and his twelve disciples ate together. During this meal, which has become known as the 'Last Supper', Jesus passed around bread and wine to his disciples, telling them that this was his body and blood, which he was about to sacrifice for the sins of mankind. Jesus commanded his followers to remember him by celebrating the supper until he returned again to the world. The people in this photograph are kneeling to receive bread and wine given to them by the priests.

SONGS OF PRAISE

Christians sing many different kinds of songs or hymns to praise God and thank him for Jesus. Adults and children who have beautiful singing voices join choirs. They sit separately at the front of the church and lead the singing. Sometimes the choir members dress in special robes and sit in seats called choir stalls. In Orthodox churches the choir and the priest sing the entire service while the worshippers stand and listen. The choir in this photograph are singing a psalm from the Bible.

SERMONS AND TALKS

This vicar is standing in a pulpit preaching to the people who have come to worship in church. Sermons, or talks, instruct their listeners how to live their lives in a Christian way. This is normally based on a passage from the Bible that has previously been read aloud to the congregation earlier in the service. Some Christians place a great emphasis on this part of their worship. They feel it is important to listen to the words of the Bible and to try and obey its teaching.

 ## CONFESSION

Confession is when Christians say sorry to God for the things they have done wrong, and so they become close to God again. This is a bit like saying sorry to a friend you have hurt so that you can be friends again. All Christians confess their sins to God and ask forgiveness.

·WHERE·DO· CHRISTIANS ·WORSHIP?·

For centuries Christians have met in beautiful buildings created especially to worship God. These can be enormous cathedrals, parish churches or tiny chapels. Some are very ornate and highly decorated, others are simple and plain. Most churches are designed to allow a group of people to meet, listen, pray, sing and celebrate together. Many churches face east, because the rising sun is a symbol of the resurrection of Jesus. The entrance to a church is often by a door facing west. In most churches there is a table called the altar. This is sometimes decorated with a cross or some candles.

CATHEDRALS

A cathedral is a very large church where large congregations of Christians meet to worship. It gets its name from the bishop's throne, or *cathedra*. Most cathedrals are very grand and impressive. This picture shows people worshipping at the Roman Catholic cathedral in London. The cathedral is highly decorated with many candles, beautiful paintings and a large crucifix hanging above the heads of the worshippers.

STAINED GLASS WINDOWS

Many churches have beautiful stained glass windows that show stories from the life of Jesus or pictures of saints. These originated at a time when many people could not read the Bible for themselves and so the stories were told to them by means of the coloured pictures all around the church. Chartres cathedral in France is famous for its stained glass windows. Modern stained glass windows are used in churches too.

Stained glass window, Chartres Cathedral

PARISH CHURCHES

The church, like this English parish church, is often the building that stands out in the community. At the west end of the church there is usually a tower or steeple that can be seen from far away. This symbolises people reaching out to God. Inside the tower there are bells that are rung to summon people to church or at special occasions like a wedding. In many churches the people sit on rows of chairs or wooden benches called pews. These face the altar, which is the focus of attention. In Orthodox churches the altar is behind a screen.

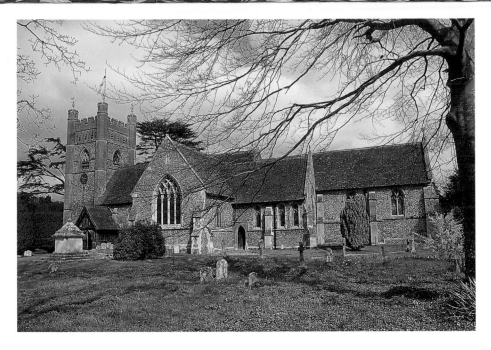

SIMPLE CHURCHES

This small African church was built out of the materials that were available in the bush. The painted cross on the wall of this building is the only thing needed to show that its members worship Jesus Christ. Wherever there are Christians, they will create a church in which to praise God. Sometimes the church may be a tent or other kind of temporary structure out of doors. The building, however, is not as important as the spirit and faith of the members.

 FREE CHURCHES

These are now often called 'Non-conformist' churches, as the members do not 'conform' to any set ritual but worship in the way they choose. Their church buildings are usually plain and simple with no statues or paintings. Some Christians meet to worship in each others' homes. These are called 'house' churches.

· W H Y · D O · CHRISTIANS · P R A Y ? ·

Prayer is the way Christians talk and listen to God. It is important for Christians to have a relationship with God and so they try to pray every day. There are different kinds of prayer. Christians pray to praise God or to say thank you for something; they pray for other people who may be sick or unhappy, or to ask for forgiveness for things they have done wrong. Sometimes Christians just talk to God about the way they feel. They believe that if it is God's will, their prayers will be answered. Christians kneel, stand, sit or lie face down on the floor to pray. Usually they put their hands together, or open them upwards to God. Some make the sign of the cross in front of their bodies.

 THE LORD'S PRAYER

Jesus taught his disciples to pray. He gave them this prayer, which is named after him. The *Lord's Prayer* contains all the different kinds of prayer (praise, request, asking for forgiveness). All Christians pray this prayer and it is used regularly in every church.

PRAYING TOGETHER

These Christian children in India are praying together at the beginning of the day before they start work. Children all over the world pray to God and sing hymns together in school assembly. In some schools the children also have lessons based on the Bible and say prayers before eating a meal. The prayer that is said before eating is a prayer of thanks for the food. This is often called 'Grace'.

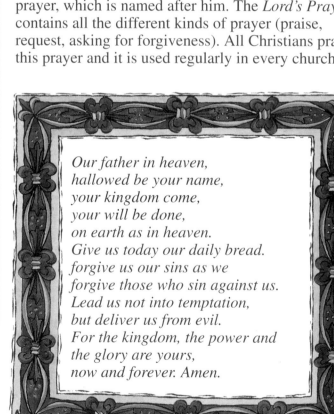

Our father in heaven,
hallowed be your name,
your kingdom come,
your will be done,
on earth as in heaven.
Give us today our daily bread.
forgive us our sins as we
forgive those who sin against us.
Lead us not into temptation,
but deliver us from evil.
For the kingdom, the power and
the glory are yours,
now and forever. Amen.

PRAYING IN CHURCH

The Christians in this church are reading the Bible and praying. The minister is looking on as a small boy leads the worship. Christians support and encourage each other by praying together. They thank God for all the good things in their lives, and for the love God gives to the world. They pray for people in their community who are sick or in trouble; Christians also pray for people in all the parts of the world who are suffering from war, famine or other disasters, and they pray for each other's problems.

PRIVATE PRAYER

Many Christians pray to God on their own for a certain time each day. They find that the more they pray, the more they are strengthened to cope with life. Some Christians light a votive (offering) candle when they say a prayer. The candle is placed in a stand near a holy statue or picture and is a visible sign of contact with God. The woman in this Orthodox Church in Russia has lit a candle and is making the sign of the cross to remind herself of how Jesus died.

PRAYER BOOK AND ROSARY

Some Christians have books or objects to help them pray. The rosary shown in the picture is a string of beads with a crucifix on the end. Beginning with the crucifix (cross) the worshipper says a prayer, then touching each bead in turn recites many other different kinds of prayers. Prayer books contain prayers written down for worshippers to read aloud.

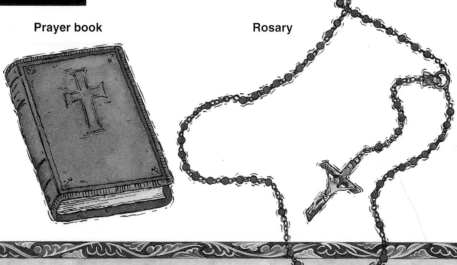

Prayer book

Rosary

All Christian believers consider themselves to be part of one enormous, international, Christian family. The members of this vast family support each other all over the world through prayer and by working together for God. Within this larger Christian family, the members also try to emphasise the importance of their own family units. Any important step in the life of a Christian is celebrated by both the immediate close family members and by the church family as a whole. The main celebrations are baptism, confirmation, first communion (celebrated by Roman Catholics), marriage and death.

BAPTISM

The first most important Christian celebration is baptism. To be baptised, a Christian is either sprinkled with, or totally submerged in, water. This symbolises the washing away of sins and the start of a new life with Jesus Christ. Jesus himself was baptised in the River Jordan and told his followers to baptise others. So baptism has always been a sign of, and a way of, becoming a Christian. Originally baptism was only for adults who chose to be baptised. The custom of baptising babies probably started during the persecution of the early Christians, when parents wanted their children to belong to Christ before they died. Nowadays infant baptism takes place at a ceremony sometimes called a 'christening'. Because babies are too young to make promises to follow Christ, they have 'godparents' to do this on their behalf. The priest in this picture is sprinkling water over the baby's forehead. He uses the baby's 'Christian' name and says, "I baptise you in the name of the Father, and of the Son, and of the Holy Spirit." Then the priest makes the sign of the cross on the baby's forehead.

CONFIRMATION

This celebration takes place when Christians 'confirm' their membership of the family of Christ in a special church service. Often the service is led by the local bishop who prays for the children or adults as they kneel before him. The bishop in this photograph anoints a boy's forehead with holy oil in the form of a cross.

 FIRST COMMUNION

For Roman Catholic children the next important step after baptism is First Communion. This takes place when the child is between the ages of seven and nine. The young child enters the church carrying a candle (often at Easter). The child is then allowed to receive Holy Communion (Mass) even though not yet confirmed.

MARRIAGE

Christians believe that marriage is a gift from God and that it is God's purpose that a husband and wife should be united in love throughout their lives, just as Jesus Christ is united in love with his church. At the marriage ceremony, called a wedding, the priest asks the couple to make solemn promises to the one they love, witnessed by others before God and with God's blessing. The couple in this picture have taken their marriage vows in front of their friends and relatives. They kneel before the vicar to be blessed.

DEATH

Although it is a very sad time when someone dies, Christians believe that a Christian who is no longer in this world has gone to heaven to be with Jesus. There, they will have no more pain and sadness, but only peace and love. Christians therefore celebrate death with prayers, hymns and Bible readings in a service called a funeral. The coffin containing the body is often cremated or buried and marked with a gravestone like this one.

A grave

WHO·ARE·THE LEADERS ·OF·THE· CHRISTIAN ·CHURCH?·

The first leaders of the Christian church were Jesus' twelve apostles. Their authority was given to them directly from Jesus. Many Christians believe that this authority has been passed down an enormous chain of church leaders through history, which therefore links modern-day leaders with the apostles. This is known as 'the apostolic succession'. When the apostles and first missionaries spread Christianity across the world, each new area of Christians had their own leader, called a patriarch (bishop). Nowadays the area of many local churches led by a bishop is called a 'diocese'. Each diocese is divided into parishes. These are in the charge of a vicar, rector or priest.

Mitre

Crozier

Robes

A Bishop of the Eastern Orthodox Church

THE POPE
This photograph is of Pope John Paul II, who is also known as the 'Bishop of Rome'. Roman Catholics believe his leadership comes directly from Peter, the apostle of Jesus who, it is thought, was the first patriarch of Rome. In the Bible it is recorded that Jesus said to Peter, "You are Peter, the Rock; and on this rock I will build my church..." Roman Catholics believe the Pope has a unique authority that no other Christian leader claims. The Pope lives in the Vatican Palace in a tiny independent state within the city of Rome.

PATRIARCHS
The Orthodox churches do not have a worldwide organisation or one supreme leader. Each Orthodox church has its own language and customs. The church is headed by a bishop called a Patriarch or 'great father'. All the Patriarchs have equal authority. Some Orthodox bishops are called 'Metropolitans'. They wear very elaborate clothing. The bishop in the picture is wearing a large hat called a mitre, and a long, embroidered cloak. He carries a 'crozier', or crook, which shows that like Jesus, he is a shepherd to his people.

ARCHBISHOP

On the right is George Carey, the Archbishop of Canterbury, who is the senior Archbishop of the Church of England and leader of the worldwide Anglican Communion. He is one of the spiritual leaders in England and has an official residence in Lambeth Palace, London, as well as in Canterbury. The actual legal 'head' of the Church of England is the Queen. Bishops and archbishops are appointed with advice from the Prime Minister. In many other countries Anglican bishops are elected by the clergy. The dioceses of the bishops are grouped together into areas called provinces. The bishop of the principal diocese may be called an archbishop.

❖ OTHER LEADERS ❖

People other than the ordained priest can lead the worship in church and preach to the congregation. These people are sometimes called lay preachers or 'elders' (because they are wise, respected members of the church). Leaders who are not ordained do not have the authority to supervise the giving of the sacraments (see page 38).

PRIESTS AND MINISTERS

This photograph shows some of the first women to be ordained as priests in the Church of England. Priests are ordained by their bishop. Then they are able to work in a parish, either as the priest in charge or as an assistant, called a curate. Once ordained, a priest can administer the Lord's Supper (Holy Communion, Mass, the Eucharist), give blessing, absolution and administer the other sacraments (see page 38). Parish priests are usually in charge of one or more churches, and they 'minister to', or serve, people who attend the church, as well as those in the local community. Priests visit the sick and elderly and help people as much as they can. Before

becoming a priest, the man or woman concerned has to train at a theological college. Then, if they are considered suitable for the role of servant and leader, they are blessed by the bishop and given the authority in a special service called 'ordination'. Sometimes parish priests are referred to as ministers. In the Free churches the word 'minister' is used instead of the term 'priest'. Both priests or ministers wear ordinary clothes or a long, plain, black coat with a white collar. Sometimes they wear a white surplice on the top. More ornate clothes, called 'vestments', are worn by some clergy (priests or ministers) when they carry out their duties.

· W H I C H · · A R E · T H E · CHRISTIAN HOLY·PLACES?

A holy place is linked in some way to the life of Christ or a Christian saint. The places in Israel where Jesus lived and worked are known as the 'Holy Land'. Other sacred places are where saints have had visions or have been buried. Christians often make journeys, called 'pilgrimages', to the places they consider holy. Sometimes people make pilgrimages in order to say special prayers of thanks or repentance. Others go to a holy place in the hope of healing and comfort. Pilgrims in the Middle Ages made long, hazardous journeys; today, modern pilgrims travel by train, coach and 'plane.

JERUSALEM

This photograph shows a view of Jerusalem, in Israel. This is a holy city for Jews, Christians and Muslims. Jerusalem was founded 3000 years ago by the Jewish king, David. Christians believe Jerusalem is the place where Jesus was crucified and rose from the dead and where God sent his Holy Spirit upon the apostles. So it is the place where the Christian Church began. Throughout history thousands of Christians have made pilgrimages to Jerusalem. When Jerusalem was captured by the Muslims in the eleventh century, the Pope at that time asked for an army to win Jerusalem back. This began a series of holy wars called the Crusades.

ST PETER'S, ROME

This is St Peter's Church, Rome. It is built on the site of the tomb of the apostle, Peter, believed to have been the first Bishop of Rome. It is thought that Peter was buried on this site after he died by crucifixion during the persecution of the Christians by the Roman Emperor, Nero. St Peter's is an enormous, Roman Catholic church full of beautiful religious paintings, sculptures and other priceless works of art, including a dome painted by the artist, Michaelangelo.

LOURDES

In 1858 a fourteen year-old girl, called Bernadette believed that she saw and talked to the Virgin Mary at Lourdes in France. After these visions, a spring of water appeared, which some people believe has healing properties. Since 1873 miraculous healings have taken place at Lourdes, and thousands of Christians like these people have made pilgrimages there in order to be healed or to gain peace of mind.

MIRACLES AND HEALING

All over the world, ever since the time of the apostles, there have been many miracles performed in the name of Jesus Christ. Throughout history, people have been healed of terrible diseases, the lame have walked and the blind have regained their sight. Some of these have happened in holy places, some have happened instantaneously, others over a period of time.

WALSINGHAM

This shrine at Walsingham in Norfolk was founded in the eleventh century by the Lady Richeldis, who had a vision of the Virgin Mary and was told to build a copy of the house of Jesus at Nazareth. The water from the well at Walsingham is believed to have the same healing power as that at Lourdes. This shrine was destroyed during the Reformation, but was restored in the twentieth century. Today it is visited by both Roman Catholics and Anglicans.

A CONVENT

The woman kneeling in this photograph is a nun taking her final vows before giving up her ordinary life to go and live in a convent. Nuns and monks give up their possessions to live in communities where they live a strict religious life of prayer and service. Nuns live in convents and monks in monasteries. Sometimes people go to stay with them for a time of quiet prayer and contemplation. This is called a 'retreat'.

·WHAT·ARE· THE·OBJECTS ·USED·IN· CHRISTIAN ·WORSHIP?·

The objects used in Christian worship vary according to the kind of church and the style of worship used and are based on the sacraments. All Christians use ritual, or special ceremonies, connected with baptism and communion. Roman Catholics and Orthodox Christians believe the bread and wine given to them at Mass actually become the body and blood of Jesus. This is called 'Transubstantiation'. Protestants believe that the bread and wine are symbols of Jesus' body and blood. The most important part of worship to Christians, however, is not the ceremony but the feeling of wanting to truly worship God, which comes from the heart.

BAPTISMAL WATER AND CANDLE
The holy water used to baptise people in many churches is kept in a container called the font. This one has a lid on it when it is not used. The candle is lit for the celebration of baptism and shows that the person has passed from darkness to light. In many Baptist churches, where people are baptised by total submersion, the water is in a pool under the floor.

 THE SACRAMENTS

A sacrament is a visible sign of something spiritual that happens to you inside. Protestants believe in the Two Sacraments commanded by Jesus. Roman Catholics and Orthodox Christians recognise seven sacraments.

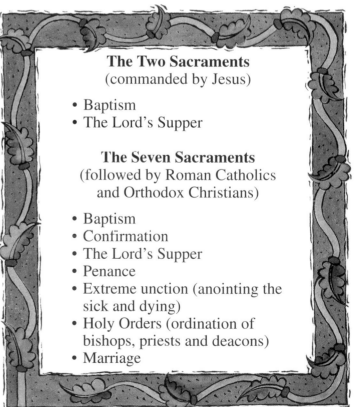

The Two Sacraments
(commanded by Jesus)

- Baptism
- The Lord's Supper

The Seven Sacraments
(followed by Roman Catholics and Orthodox Christians)

- Baptism
- Confirmation
- The Lord's Supper
- Penance
- Extreme unction (anointing the sick and dying)
- Holy Orders (ordination of bishops, priests and deacons)
- Marriage

BREAD AND WINE

This photograph is of the chalice and paten which are the cup and plate used to hold the bread and wine in the celebration of the Lord's Supper (see page 26). The chalice holds the wine, which represents the blood of Jesus Christ. The paten holds the 'host' (bread or wafers), which represent his body. Some churches use a wafer to represent the unleavened bread (bread that has not risen) eaten by the Jews in the Passover Meal. Other churches, including the Orthodox church believe that the Last Supper was the night before the Passover, so they use ordinary bread. In some Protestant churches grape-juice or non-alcoholic wine is used instead of real wine.

INCENSE

Some Christians use incense in their services. This symbolises their prayers rising to God. Incense is made from the resin of trees, and when crystals of it are spread on smouldering charcoal, a sweet-smelling smoke is produced as they burn.

The incense is carried in a thurible.

HOLY OIL

Throughout history the use of oil for anointing people in the name of God has had special significance. The prophets of ancient Israel anointed the people chosen by God to be kings of Israel. Holy oil is still used today. This priest is anointing a sick person with oil that has been blessed by the bishop. This is called the 'sacrament of unction'. Some Christians use oil at baptism to dedicate the child to God. This is called 'chrismation'. Holy oil is sometimes used by a priest or bishop to make the sign of the cross on those being confirmed.

· DO · CHRISTIANS · HAVE · A · TRADITION · OF · MUSIC-MAKING?

Throughout history Christians have used music and song in the worship and praise of God, and to celebrate the birth and resurrection of Jesus Christ. This music takes many forms. Many brilliant composers have felt inspired by God to create spectacular 'masses', beautiful hymns and melodious chants. Many Anglican and Roman Catholic churches have traditional hymns and psalms as part of the service. Pentecostals and Charismatics place a great emphasis on contemporary songs of praise accompanied by a music group with electric guitars. Orthodox Christians do not use instruments. They rely on the singing of the priest and choir to lead the worship. Some Christians such as the Society of Friends do not use any music in their worship at all.

GREGORIAN CHANTS

These monks are chanting 'plainsong' together. This is music unaccompanied by instruments and is probably how the Christians of the Early Church worshipped together. The melodic, unaccompanied chanting is often called 'Gregorian' chant, named after Pope Gregory the Great who died in CE604. Gregory was famous for the choirs and choral scholars he established in Roman churches. Much of the music composed in the style of plainsong is attributed to Pope Gregory even though a large amount of it was composed after his death.

CHOIRS

Choirs have been known since the fourth century CE. In many churches a choir joins in with the singing of the congregation and also sings alone. The choir is usually drawn from the congregation, but many cathedrals have their own professional choristers like those shown in the photograph. These are often male choirs, although today mixed choirs are becoming more common. Composers such as Mozart, Haydn, Bach, Handel and Britten composed great musical works to be sung in church, but they are also performed by many choirs in large concert halls.

ORGAN MUSIC

Organs have been used as instruments to accompany singing in church since the Middle Ages. The grandiose sound made by the reverberating organ pipes makes it an ideal instrument for a large building such as a church, with the advantage that only one person is needed to play the keyboards. The eighteenth-century musican Bach was a brilliant organist and composer. He created hundreds of musical works and organ pieces. Many churches have an organ which is used to play music before, during and after the end of church services.

Church organ

GOSPEL MUSIC

The singers in the photograph above are Gospel Singers. This is a kind of hymn-singing that began in the USA around 1870. By 1930, Black Gospel music had developed its own style and is especially associated with the Pentecostal churches. It is a mixture of old hymns and elements from spiritual songs.

The singers often sway or dance back and forth, clapping their hands, accompanied by the sound of organ, piano, tambourine and electric guitars. Often the bass voice echoes the other parts. Black Gospel music is performed by many Christians and has been incorporated into church services of many denominations.

THE SALVATION ARMY

This worldwide Christian organisation began as a Christian mission in a poor part of London. It was founded in 1878 by a Methodist preacher, William Booth, and his wife Catherine, who both wanted a Christian army to fight against sin and poverty. The Salvation Army now helps the poor and homeless everywhere. William Booth wanted to bring into his services an informal atmosphere that would put new members at their ease. So there is an emphasis on joyful singing, instrumental music and hand-clapping. The rousing hymn-singing often takes place outside to attract crowds to listen to the word of God.

· DO · CHRISTIANS · HAVE · A · TRADITION · OF · STORYTELLING?

The stories from the Holy Bible have been passed down through the generations by word of mouth and in ancient manuscripts for over 2000 years. Many of them are stories of peoples' lives, their joys and fears and their tragedies and battles. Some are very exciting, dramatic and beautiful. Christians believe the stories in the Bible show people what God is like. For most Christians the greatest story in the Bible is the life of Jesus: his birth, crucifixion and resurrection from the dead. But also there are the stories that Jesus himself told. Some of these stories are called 'parables'.

NATIVITY PLAYS

These children are acting in a Christmas nativity play. This is a play about the story of Jesus Christ's birth. The children are dressed up as Mary, Joseph and the shepherds who came to visit the baby Jesus in the stable where he was born. Every year Christian children all over the world tell the Christmas story to others in this way.

PARABLES

Like many Jewish teachers, Jesus Christ was a marvellous storyteller. When he was teaching people about God and trying to explain about God, Jesus sometimes told stories called 'parables'. A parable is often called 'an earthly story with a heavenly meaning'. It is a story about things that happen in everyday life, but for those who are really listening and understanding there is also a second, deeper meaning. Jesus used this kind of storytelling to help ordinary people understand and remember the main point of his teaching.

One of the more well-known parables that Jesus told is the Parable of the Sower, which is told on the next page. You can find this in the eighth chapter of St Luke, in the New Testament section of the Holy Bible.

THE PARABLE OF THE SOWER

One day when Jesus was teaching by the Sea of Galilee, there were so many people gathered along the shore he decided to climb into a boat and preach to the crowd from there. First of all, he told them the parable of the sower.

"Listen to this," he said. There was once a farmer who went out to sow his seed in the fields. As he scattered the seed around him, some seed fell on the path. The birds saw it and quickly swooped down and ate it up."

"Other seed fell on rocky places where there wasn't much soil. It sprang up quickly but couldn't put down roots because the soil was shallow. So, when the hot sun shone down on the little shoots, they withered and died."

"Some seed fell amongst thorns. When the plants grew up, the thorns choked them, so they could not bear fruit."

"Then there was the seed that fell on good soil. It took root, grew up strong and produced a good harvest."

When Jesus had finished the story, he said, "You have all got ears, now use them and listen well."

But the followers of Jesus who were close by were puzzled. "We don't understand what you're saying," they told him.

Jesus said to them, "I use stories to explain about God, so that those who are really interested in the Lord will listen carefully, think about the story and understand it. Those who don't want to find out the truth won't bother to look for the meaning, and will be left in the dark." Then he explained the parable to the apostles.

"The farmer is the teacher, or person who spreads God's message. The seed is the word of God. Some people are like the seed sown along the path. As soon as they hear the word of God, the Devil comes along and makes them forget all about it."

"Other people are like the seed sown on rocky ground. They hear God's message and receive it happily, but as their belief is not deep-rooted, they soon give up on God when others tease or hurt them because of their faith."

"Then there are those like the seed that falls amongst thorns. They hear God's message, and want to live his way, but soon all their other desires and worries take over and push God out of their thoughts.

"Finally," said Jesus, "there are those people who are like the seed sown on good soil. They hear God's message and take it into their hearts. Their belief is deep-rooted and strong, so they live a good life and show others that they are obeying God."

·GLOSSARY·

ABSOLUTION A prayer said by a priest to a person who has confessed their sins, done a penance (see below) and has been forgiven. The prayer of absolution tells the person they are forgiven for their wrongdoings.

ANGEL A heavenly being. The word angel comes from the Greek word for messenger and in many Bible stories angels delivered messages from God.

APOSTLE The name given to the disciples chosen by Jesus to continue the work that he did and to whom he gave his authority.

CANONISATION The procedure that has to be gone through before someone is made a saint. Another person has to try to find faults with the writings or actions of the saintly person to try to prove that he or she is not perfect. The person finding the fault is called 'devil's advocate'. If no fault can be found, the person is made a saint.

CRUCIFIXION A very cruel form of execution used by the ancient Romans for common criminals. The victim was nailed or tied to a wooden cross and left to die in the heat of the sun.

DEVIL Christians believe that the Devil (also called Satan) is the enemy of God and the source of all evil.

DISCIPLE A follower (of Jesus Christ). At first Jesus chose twelve disciples. Later he had many followers.

EPISTLE The name given to a long letter. When he was in prison Paul wrote long letters to encourage, advise and help all the new Christians whom he had converted on his missionary journeys.

FASTING Going without food for a period of time. Christians often fast or give up some kind of food during Lent. This reminds them of the time when Jesus fasted and prayed to God before he began his work, and makes Christians understand a little of what Jesus went through.

FRANKINCENSE A very expensive strong-smelling incense used in the East for burning at special ceremonies.

GOD Christians believe that God is the one, eternal source of goodness and love.

HOLY TRINITY Christians believe in one God who has revealed himself to the world as Father, Son (Jesus) and Holy Spirit (which came at Pentecost). These are not three different gods but different sorts of activity by God through which he makes contact with the people and world he created.

INCARNATION The process by which God the Son became human in Jesus. Almost all Christians believe that Jesus was both God and also human.

MYRRH A strong-smelling resin used in incense, perfume and medicine.

PALESTINE In Bible times this is the name given by the ancient Romans to the area previously known as Canaan. It was where the Jewish nation lived in the time of Jesus.

PENANCE Something that is done by people to show that they are sorry for their sins. Often this is a Bible reading or prayer given by a priest to a person. When this is done, the person shows that he or she has repented of (said sorry for) the sins. This is one of the seven sacraments.

PERSECUTE To kill, injure or harrass someone, usually because of what they believe in.

REPENTANCE When a person says sorry to God for all the things he or she has done wrong in the past. People ask God to help them live a better life.

SECOND COMING Christians believe that this is the time when Jesus will come into the world again to judge people on how they have lived their lives. Christians also believe that, when this happens, the world as we know it will end and there will be no more pain or sadness for those who trust in God.

SECOND TEMPLE The temple that was built after the Jews returned from exile in Babylon. The first temple (built by King Solomon) was destroyed with the city of Jerusalem by King Nebuchadnezzar of Babylon.

SIN Another word for wrongdoing. It is something people do that is unloving and against God's laws. Christians believe sin harms their relationship with God.

SLAV COUNTRIES Places where people spoke Slavonic. Slavonia used to be a region of North Yugoslavia.

'SPEAKING IN TONGUES' The ability to speak in other languages that have not been learnt. This ability is given to Christians instantly by the Holy Spirit coming into them, enabling them to communicate with God more directly.

SYRIAC An ancient language used by Roman Syrians.

UNCTION When a person is anointed with holy oil, usually by a bishop or priest. The reason for this is to give strength to that person through the Holy Spirit. It is often done when someone is very ill or dying (extreme unction), which is one of the seven sacraments.

VISION A supernatural image that appears in front of someone. For Christians the vision is usually one of Jesus, the Virgin Mary or Christian saints.

· I N D E X ·